Awesum Alex
Math Detective

The Addition Problem

Rachel R. McAnallen

Illustrations by Christopher Tice

Royal Fireworks Press
Unionville, New York

Royal Fireworks Press
P.O. Box 399
41 First Avenue
Unionville, NY 10988-0399
(845) 726-4444
fax: (845) 726-3824
email: mail@rfwp.com
website: rfwp.com

ISBN: 978-0-89824-634-6

Printed and bound in Unionville, New York, on acid-free paper
using vegetable-based inks at the Royal Fireworks facility.

Publisher: Dr. T.M. Kemnitz
Editor: Jennifer Ault
Book and cover designer: Christopher Tice

22spt17

Alex Hypatia was a thinker.

No matter where she was or what she was doing, Alex was always thinking. And what she liked to think about best were numbers, shapes, and patterns. She loved to count in all sorts of different ways.

If a cheek-pinching grown-up asked her, "How old are you, young lady?" Alex was inclined to answer importantly, "One hundred fifteen!" This was not a fib; she was 115, after all—if you counted in months. Alex thought with a smile, "If they want my answer in years, they should say so."

Even when she was eating she found numbers to play with, which explains why Alex sat at the breakfast table playing "Marshmallow Math" with her cereal on the first day of school.

She took her spoon and ate all six orange pentagons first. Since pentagons have five sides, they were worth five points each. "Five, ten, fifteen, twenty, twenty-five, thirty sides," Alex munched to herself. Next she ate five blue squares: "Four, eight, twelve, sixteen, twenty sides." Then she ate five yellow triangles: "Three, six, nine, twelve, fifteen sides." Finally she ate the oat circles, and since they didn't have sides, they were zeros. "Zero, zero, zero, zero…plus zero, zero, zero, zero." It was a challenge holding the other numbers in her head while she ate all those zeros. "Zero…plus zero, zero, zero…ZERO!"

The thirty sides of the six pentagons, plus the twenty sides of the five squares, added to the fifteen sides of the five triangles, plus all the zeroes, came to a total of sixty-five sides. "Sixty-five!" she announced to her family.

"You're going to get along great with Mrs. Googol-Plex," Alex's older sister Grace informed her. "She turns everything into a game."

Alex agreed. Everybody at Emmy Noether Elementary knew that Mrs. Googol-Plex was the world's most creative fifth-grade teacher. She rode a motorcycle to school and wore red cowboy boots. Her classroom was often full of noise and excitement.

Alex's father handed Alex a brown paper lunch bag. "Lettuce, tomato, and Swiss cheese, as requested," he said with a smile. Swiss cheese was Alex's favorite. Not only was it tasty; there were ellipses for her to count. Over the summer she had eaten a total of 723 ellipses in thirty-two sandwiches.

On the way to school, Alex's best friend Thomas helped her count how many vehicles they passed. By the time the bus pulled into the schoolyard, they had counted twenty-seven cars, nine trucks, four bicycles, and two scooters. They only counted one motorcycle.

They also had fun playing the license plate game to see how many different ways they could add up the numbers on a license plate. They saw a plate from Illinois and had a contest to see how many different ways they could add the numbers.

Alex yelled out, "I see an 8 and a 2, so that makes 10. Then I see a 6 and a 2 and another 2, so that makes another 10, and that added to the first 10 makes a 20. There is a 6 remaining, so the total is 26!"

Thomas said, “I got 26 another way. I saw that 2 plus 2 plus 8 is 12; then 6 plus 6 is another 12. So 12 plus 12 is 24, plus the last number 2 is 26.”

A girl named Wu Li piped up and said, “I love 6’s, so I added the three 2’s and got 6. I broke the 8 into 6 plus 2, so that meant that I had four 6’s, which is 24, and adding the 2 left over from the 8 makes 26.”

Alex's stomach did 360-degree spins as she and Thomas climbed the steps that led to the fifth- and sixth-grade section of the school. They searched for their new classroom together. "Not this one," said Alex thankfully when they peeked into the first room at the top of the stairs. It was silent, empty, and dull.

The next room wasn't dull at all. Colorful models and spinning mobiles hung from the ceiling. On the walls there were bright posters with pictures of interesting shapes, labeled with long names like "Stellated Icosahedron." Alex noticed that there was a number line over the board that had positive and negative numbers on it instead of the alphabet. Instead of plain boring rows, the desks formed a semicircle in the center of the room. "This must be it!" she exclaimed.

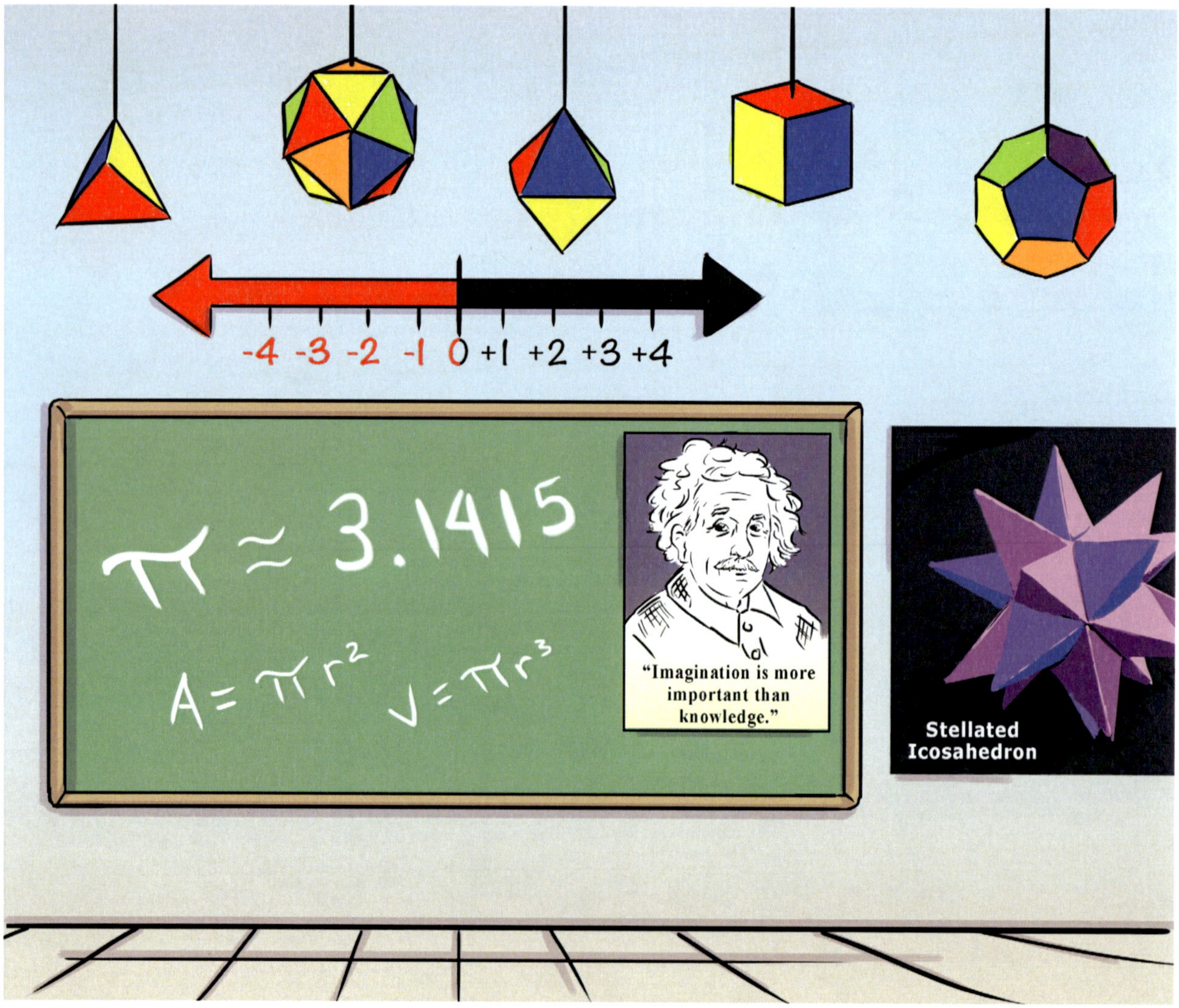

As if on cue, Mrs. Googol-Plex appeared in the doorway. Her hair was a wild tangle of orange curls, and it framed a smiling face. "Come on in!" she said. "Welcome to our classroom!"

It was a wonderfully busy morning, full of what Mrs. Googol-Plex liked to call "productive sound." But of course what Alex enjoyed most was math class.

"Math is simply finding out how much or how many," said Mrs. Googol-Plex. "Addition is just sophisticated counting. Subtraction is sophisticated counting backwards. Multiplication is sophisticated addition, and division is sophisticated subtraction."

"Think outside the box," Mrs. Googol-Plex told them with a smile.

Think outside the box? Alex envisioned her brain sitting on top of a cardboard box, but that didn't make much sense. So she asked, "What does that mean, Mrs. Googol-Plex?"

"What do you think it means?" answered her teacher.

Alex wondered if anyone else was imagining a brain on top of a box. "I'm not sure," she answered honestly.

Mrs. Googol-Plex wasn't concerned if a person didn't know the answer right away. "That's okay," she said. "I like to give plenty of think time."

Mrs. Googol-Plex wrote the following numbers on the board:

$$\begin{array}{r} +\ 123 \\ +\ 234 \\ \underline{+\ 321} \end{array}$$

"How would you add these numbers?" she asked. "Where would you start?"

Thomas raised his hand. "Add 3 plus 4 plus 1," he said quickly.

"Add the digits in the ones column first! That sounds reasonable!" said Mrs. Googol-Plex. "Does anyone else have another way?"

"Could we add the tens column first?" asked Wu Li.

"No one ever adds the tens first," said Thomas.

"What about adding the hundreds column first?" Alex suggested.

"No way!" said Thomas. "You can't do that!"

"There is a difference between ***place*** value and ***face*** value."

Alex frowned. "Do we always have to add the ones first, Mrs. Googol-Plex?" she asked.

"Yes," Thomas piped up. "My dad told me you always start with the ones column."

"I was asking Mrs. Googol-Plex, not you," Alex told her friend indignantly.

"It appears that we've stumbled upon our first Math Mystery of the school year!" said Mrs. Googol-Plex with a wide smile. Alex wiggled her toes with excitement. She loved mysteries!

"Think of yourselves as detectives—math detectives," Mrs. Googol-Plex continued. "I want everyone to be on the lookout for clues. Think about order and how it relates to adding the ones column, the tens column, and the hundreds column."

"This should be easy. I already know the answer," Thomas whispered to Alex. Alex ignored him.

"The evidence is all around you, so be alert!" advised Mrs. Googol-Plex. "I'll even give you a clue toward solving the case," she said, leaning forward a bit. "There is a difference between place value and face value."

For rest of the day, Alex's mind kept wandering back to the Math Mystery. She was sure that it was possible to add the hundreds column first; she just had to find a way to prove it. "There is a difference between face value and place value," she repeated to herself. "What does that mean?"

Alex and Thomas had planned to walk home after school so they could talk about their first day. As they walked down the sidewalk, Alex paused outside a shop with a sign that read: Random's Variety Store. "If I'm going to solve the Math Mystery, I need to have the proper tools," she told Thomas. "I'm going to get a special notebook and some pencils."

Alex opened the door. When she and Thomas stepped inside the store, their jaws dropped. They stared in amazement at the jungle of hammers and potholders, jump ropes and watering cans, potato ricers and adjustable wrenches that appeared before them. From ceiling to floor, the store was an endless tangle of gadgets and doohickeys. Nothing was in order.

VOL
SALE
BIG BOX

"Yikes!" said Thomas. Alex wandered hopefully down an aisle marked "School Supplies." Instead of finding pencils, she found eggbeaters. Instead of notebooks, she found fuzzy slippers.

"Can I help you?" asked a voice from somewhere within the store. Mr. Random appeared from behind a rubber raft that was blocking the register.

"Yes, I'm looking for a notebook and some pencils, please," Alex said politely.

Mr. Random scratched his head. "Ah, yes. Let me think.... Where on earth did I put the pencils?"

Mr. Random began to search through a barrel filled with all sorts of odds and ends. "They must be here somewhere," he muttered to himself, tossing a tennis racket aside. Alex and Thomas exchanged puzzled glances. A hula hoop, a beach ball, and a sneaker all flew though the air.

"I have to be home before dark," Thomas hissed as he dodged a projectile rubber ducky.

"Uh, Mr. Random? Wouldn't it be easier to find the pencils if you kept them all together in the School Supplies aisle?" Alex asked him. But he was too busy digging to hear her.

"Found the pencils!" Mr. Random suddenly yelled from the depths of the barrel. He emerged waving a package of pencils. "See? I knew they were here somewhere!"

"Um, never mind about the notebook," said Alex. "I'll just take these."

"That will be $1.00," he told Alex.

"Thank you," said Alex, handing him the money.

"Have a nice day!" said Mr. Random cheerfully.

Random's
Variety Store
Register
CASH ONLY
Pencils

"Wouldn't it have been easier if he kept everything in its place?" Alex whispered to Thomas as they left the store.

"Hopeless!" Thomas whispered back.

"And I still need a notebook!" said Alex. "Let's try another store."

"No thanks!" said Thomas firmly. "I'll wait outside!"

The next shop was orderly. Alex walked down the clearly marked aisles, quickly found a notebook, and paid for it.

"That was much faster," said Thomas when she met him on the sidewalk.

"Having things in their proper place makes a big difference!" said Alex.

At dinner that night, Alex told her family about her day. "Our homework is to be math detectives," she explained. "We are investigating whether you always have to add the ones column first."

Alex's mother was particularly interested in the assignment. She worked at a bank and was well-acquainted with adding numbers together. "I think I will invite Mrs. Googol-Plex to bring your class to the bank," she said. "There's no better place to investigate numbers."

"Excellent!" said Alex's father.

"Pretty neat," admitted Grace, Alex's sister.

"Good idea," said Alex with a grin.

After supper was over and the dishes were washed, it was Alex's chore to put them away. "What should I put away first: plates, cups, or silverware?" she asked her mother.

"It doesn't matter what you put away first, so long as all the clean stuff ends up in its correct place," her mother replied.

Alex remembered Mr. Random's store. What if she began to cram the dinner plates into the silverware drawer or made a giant pile of forks in the cupboard?

While she put the plates away, Alex thought about the addition problem that Mrs. Googol-Plex had written on the board. "Place value is different than face value," she chanted. But the clue didn't seem to be helping. "I just need more think time," she told herself.

The next afternoon, Mrs. Googol-Plex announced, "Math class is being held at the bank today. Mrs. Hypatia has invited us do some hands-on investigative work."

Alex's mother showed them all around the bank. "At the bank, we use numbers to describe how much money we have," she explained. "When someone comes into the bank to withdraw money, they don't say, 'I would like to withdraw 234.' They say, 'I would like to withdraw 234 *dollars*.'"

"How do you count it?" asked Alex.

"Like this," Mrs. Hypatia answered. She laid two one hundred-dollar bills on the counter: "One hundred, two hundred." Next she counted out three ten-dollar bills: "Ten, twenty, thirty." Last of all she laid down the one-dollar bills: "One, two, three, four. A total of 234 dollars," she announced.

Alex's eyes widened. She stared at the one-dollar bills on the counter in front of her. Her mother had counted them last! And she had counted the one hundred-dollar bills first!

"Do you always count the biggest bills first?" she asked eagerly.

"Yes," said Mrs. Hypatia. "It is easier to start with the hundreds and finish with the ones. When you work with one hundred-dollar bills, you are counting by hundreds. When you work with twenty-dollar bills, you are counting by twenties. When you work with ten-dollar bills, you are counting by tens. Five-dollar bills mean you count by fives. And last of all you count by ones," she explained. "It's a more efficient way to count your money."

"In mathematics, we call that counting in descending order," said Mrs. Googol-Plex. "That means we start high and end low. Think about how you say numbers," she told the children. "Alex, say a three-digit number for me."

"One hundred twenty-three," said Alex.

One hundred twenty-three!
MATH
Welc

“Think about it,” Mrs. Googol-Plex urged. “What number came out of your mouth first?

“One hundred,” said Alex.

“And what number came out of your mouth second?”

“Twenty,” answered Alex.

“And what did you say last?”

“Three,” Alex replied.

“Well, that’s in descending order!” Mrs. Googol-Plex said. “We are saying the math sentence in descending order: one hundred plus twenty plus three.”

Mrs. Googol-Plex held up a twenty-dollar bill and a five-dollar bill. “How much do I have?”

“Twenty-five,” said Alex.

“Twenty-five *what*?” asked Mrs. Googol-Plex.

“Twenty-five dollars.”

“That’s right!” she said. “No matter what order you count them in, having a five-dollar bill and a twenty-dollar bill is twenty-five dollars. That is called the Commutative Property of Addition.”

Commutative Property of Addition:

20 + 5 = 5 + 20

“When we add our bills together,” Mrs. Googol-Plex continued, “we can start counting with any bill that I’m holding. No matter where we start, we still have twenty-five dollars.”

"It also doesn't matter in what order you add the numbers," Mrs. Googol-Plex went on. "We can add in any order we want: ones, tens, or hundreds first. That's called the Associative Property of Addition."

Associative Property of Addition:

$$100 + 10 + 1 = 100 + 1 + 10$$

$$=$$

$$10 + 100 + 1 = 10 + 1 + 100$$

$$=$$

$$1 + 100 + 10 = 1 + 10 + 100$$

"So we did it!" said Alex. "We solved the Math Mystery!"

"True," agreed Mrs. Googol-Plex. "We have proven that we can add things in any order. I heard that you play an addition game with license plates. Did you know you were using the Associative Property of Addition when you added up those numbers?"

"Is there more we need to know?" asked Alex.

"True mathematicians must be able to prove their cases on paper. To solve our mystery fully, we need to justify our answer."

"How do we do that?" puzzled Alex.

"It has to do with your clue," answered Mrs. Googol-Plex. "Place value is different than face value. Think about it, and we will talk more about it in class tomorrow."

Alex scribbled furiously in her notebook. "I just have to figure out this clue!" she said to herself.

Alex thought about the Math Mystery. She thought and thought and thought, right up until she fell asleep that night. "Think outside the box," she mumbled as she drifted off. "Place value is different than face value…."

Place value is different than **face value**...

Alex awoke feeling cramped and hot. "It can't be morning," she thought. "It's too dark." Then she noticed that her bed felt hard…and her covers were gone…and so was her pillow….

She tried to sit up, and THUMP! She banged her head and her elbow at the same time.

Alex felt around and counted, "One wall, two walls, three walls, four… plus a ceiling and a floor…a cube!" she whispered. "I'm all boxed in!"

She was in a very uncomfortable predicament. "I hope this thing opens!" Alex reached up and pushed as hard as she could. The top flipped open with a whoosh. She stood sleepily and rubbed her eyes.

It was obvious that she was no longer in her bedroom. She wasn't even in her house—or even, it seemed, in her neighborhood. "This is very strange," Alex observed as she climbed from the box and stepped onto firm ground. "I wonder where I am?"

Polyhedra Palace 5 miles
Fraction Forest THIS WAY
Base Ten Town ONE MILE

Then she noticed a signpost covered with arrows and names of places. "Polyhedra Palace, 5 miles," read Alex. "Fraction Forest, this way. Base Ten Town, one mile." But she had never heard of any of those places.

"Now what?" Alex asked aloud. She was not actually expecting anyone to answer her.

"Maybe I can help," boomed an enthusiastic voice.

Alex jumped in surprise. "Who said that?"

"I did, of course!" said the voice. "Who else?"

Alex looked all around her, but she didn't see anyone—not even a bug.

"Up here!" the voice shouted impatiently. "On the post!"

Alex looked, and sure enough, there at the top of the signpost stood a tiny person tapping her tiny feet.

"Are you the Tooth Fairy?" Alex asked.

"The Tooth Fairy?" The tiny figure put her hand on her hip. "Certainly not!"

"Well, what are you, then?" asked Alex inquisitively.

The tiny figure straightened herself up and said grandly, "It just so happens that I am a *guru*! A math guru, to be exact!"

"O-oh…sorry," Alex apologized. "But I still don't understand."

"I'm a powerful mathematician! I might be a little on the short side, but I push around some very big numbers!"

"Wow," said Alex.

Fibonacci
EXPRESS

"I also do a little investigative work on the side," added Alex's new acquaintance. "Detective Martha-Matrix, PI, at your service. Word on the street is you've got a Math Mystery to solve."

"You don't look like a detective," said Alex reluctantly.

"Of course not!" scoffed the miniature mathematician. "I'm a master of disguise! And if you want to be a math detective, the first thing you need to learn is that you can't judge everything by its face value."

"Face value? That's part of the clue!" said Alex. "Maybe you really can help me!"

"Now you're catching on, kid!" Martha-Matrix floated down off the signpost and landed on Alex's shoulder. "Let's hop on the Fibonacci Express and slide into town! There are some people you need to meet if we're going to solve your mystery."

The Fibonacci Express was a giant slide that twirled and swirled and luckily had a soft landing at the bottom. Alex stood up and regained her balance on another signpost, which declared, "Welcome to Base Ten Town, Population 10^{100}."

"Phew, what a ride!" huffed the petite PI, straightening her clothes. "I hope you don't mind providing my transportation while you're here. I prefer flying, but," she looked at Alex, "I assume that you don't fly at all?"

"No, not without an airplane," Alex admitted.

"Well, then, I guess you'll have to do," sighed Martha-Matrix, drifting up and settling once more on Alex's shoulder. "Otherwise you couldn't keep up with me. Just take the first left on this road here," she directed. "Circle H Ranch."

"A ranch?" asked Alex. "But aren't we going into town?"

"Yes," Martha-Matrix assured her, "but first we have to visit some friends who live out on the range. It won't take long. Look, you can see them from here."

A few yards away, Alex could see a huddle of large, square figures in cowboy hats seated around a campfire.

"Don't worry," Martha-Matrix reassured Alex in a low voice. "These cowboys are the Hundreds Gang. They may look like tough characters, but they're perfectly friendly."

"Mornin', Miz Number Lady!" one of the cowboys hollered with a wave of his hat. "What are you doin' in these here parts?"

"Howdy, pardners!" thundered the small but loud companion on Alex's shoulder. "I was wondering if I could round up a few of you cowpokes to join in on a math rodeo!"

"Sure thing! We'd be mighty pleased to lend a hand!" drawled a cowgirl.

"Great!" said Martha-Matrix. "I'll need six of you to mosey over to the intersection of X and Y. We'll meet you there!"

"But how are cowboys going to help me with my Math Mystery?" Alex wondered aloud.

"Don't worry," Martha-Matrix reassured her. "You'll see!"

WELCOME
to
Base Ten
Town

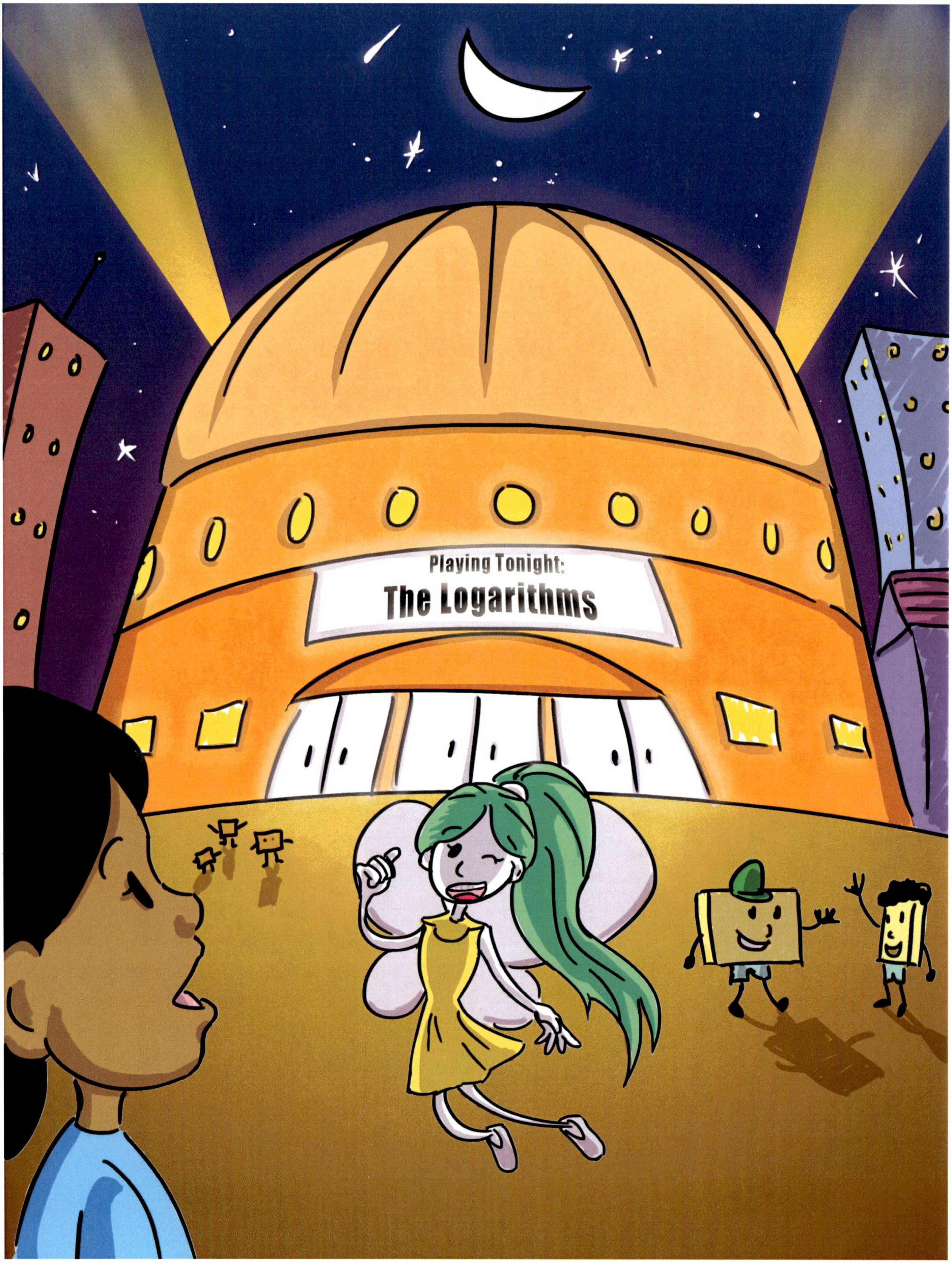
Playing Tonight:
The Logarithms

As they walked through Base Ten Town, Martha-Matrix pointed out the sites for Alex. "There's the Geometry Garden Café—best food in Calculus County. Algebra Alley is that way. And here's our next stop: the Decimal Dome!"

"It looks like a sports arena," said Alex in a puzzled tone.

"Of course!" replied her tiny tour guide. "Where else would you find basketball players? Terrific team, the Base Ten Town Tens. They're having a great season!"

Alex followed her guide onto the court, where several tall, skinny block figures were practicing their lay-ups. Martha-Matrix, master of disguise, blew a referee's whistle to get the team's attention. "Listen up! I need seven of you players to hustle over to the intersection of X and Y! We've got an important math game to play!"

"Okay, Coach, we'll give it our best shot!" yelled one of the players.

"Great! I'll catch you later!" said Martha-Matrix.

PLAYING TONIGHT:
Count Base
&
The Ones Orchestra

"Cowboys and basketball players?" pondered Alex as they walked back out onto the street. "What's next?"

"We're off to the Tangent Theater!" Martha-Matrix replied gleefully. "Way off at the edge of town!"

Music with a catchy beat was pouring out onto the street from the Tangent Theater. "Little guys with a big band sound," said Martha-Matrix, snapping her fingers in time.

The musicians rehearsing on the stage were small and cube-shaped. Count Base signaled the Ones to stop playing when he saw Alex and Martha-Matrix. "Look, everyone. It's the Maestro of Math!" he called. "Any requests?"

"No requests, but how about a favor?" asked Martha-Matrix.

"Anything for you," said the Count.

"I was wondering if you and seven of your band members could swing on over to the intersection of X and Y for a little math concert. It's for a case I'm working on."

"Sounds like a fun gig!" said Count Base. "We'll be there."

It wasn't long before Alex and Martha-Matrix joined a crowd of block people assembled at the intersection of X and Y.

"Okay!" Martha-Matrix called out. "Thank you all for coming this evening!" She turned to Alex. "It's time to recreate the scene! Give me the numbers involved in your Math Mystery."

"One hundred twenty-three, plus two hundred thirty-four, plus three hundred twenty-one," Alex answered. "But what do you mean 'recreate the scene'?"

"Simple," said Martha-Matrix. "Our friends here are going help you solve that pesky clue about face value and place value. They are here to represent your numbers!"

"How?" Alex asked, still not sure she understood.

"You'll notice that the cowboys are each made up of 100 blocks," explained Martha-Matrix. "We'll call them hundreds. The basketball players are each made up of ten blocks. We'll call them tens. The musicians are just single blocks. We'll call them ones. Together they make all sorts of numbers!" She called out loudly, "Attention! Please form the following groups as I call them!"

The crowd murmured agreeably.

X ST
Y ST

“Could I see the number 123, please!” shouted Martha-Matrix. One cowhand, two basketball players, and three musicians congregated together.

“Nice!” said Martha. “Next, I need 234!” Two cowhands, three basketball players, and four musicians gathered into another bunch.

"Lovely! Finally, can I have 321?" Three cowboys, two basketball players, and one musician formed a line.

The math guru pointed at the crowd. "Who do you see first?" she asked Alex.

Scattered throughout, the hulking forms of the cowboy blocks stood out among the rest. "I see six cowboys, worth 100 blocks each. So I see six hundreds."

"Good! Then what do you see?"

"I see seven basketball players," answered Alex. "That would be seven tens."

"And then what?"

"I see eight musicians," Alex said, counting carefully. "That's eight ones."

hundreds
tens
ones
2 2 2
200 + 20 + 2

"Exactly!" said Martha-Matrix. "Let's look at something." She called out to the group, "I need 222 over here!" Two cowboys, two basketball players, and two musicians walked over and stood in front of Alex.

"In the real world, numbers are represented using digits," said Martha-Matrix. With a wave of her staff, the digits 0 though 9 appeared and floated above them. "Digits have face value."

"These digits make up all the numbers we use every day," explained Martha-Matrix. "Numbers describe how much you have of something. Knowing how much you have of something depends on where the digit is placed. Numbers have place value."

With a wave of her staff, the digits disappeared. With another flourish of the wand, three 2's appeared in the air above them.

"What number does this set of digits represent?" she asked Alex.

Alex thought carefully. "Two hundred twenty-two," she answered.

"Correct!" said Martha-Matrix. "The face value of all these digits is two, but each one has a different place value."

Martha-Matrix pointed to the 2 on the far left. What is the place value of this digit?" she asked Alex.

"Two hundred," answered Alex. The two cowboys in front of her linked arms and did a little jig. In their enthusiasm, they almost squished a little musician under their feet.

Martha-Matrix pointed up to the digit in the middle. "And what is the place value of this digit?"

"Twenty," said Alex. The basketball players grinned and gave each other high fives.

Martha-Matrix pointed to the digit on the far right. "Now, what is the place value of this digit?"

"Two," answered Alex. The tiny musicians, who had moved far away from the cowboys' feet, each gave a bow.

"Exactly!" exclaimed Martha-Matrix. "As you can see, we should *never* call a 200 or a 20 a 2! Why? Our friend Cowboy Hundred is 100 times bigger than Count Base!"

Cowboy Hundred puffed up a bit at this, until Martha-Matrix added firmly, "That doesn't make him better, of course, but it does mean that he needs to watch where he plants his big clodhoppers!"

"That's the clue! Place value *is* different than face value!" shouted Alex. "It finally makes sense!"

"Absolutely!" said Martha-Matrix. "Do you ever call an A a Z?"

"No!" said Alex.

"Do you ever call an M a W?"

"Never!" replied Alex.

"And are you ever going to confuse a great big galute like Cowboy Hundred with a talented little guy like Count Base?"

"No way!" shouted Alex.

"Then raise your hand and repeat what I like to call 'The Math Detective Oath,'" instructed the tiny teacher. "I promise always to call numbers by their correct place value names."

"I promise always to call numbers by their correct place value names," Alex repeated solemnly as the crowd cheered her on. She meant every word.

"I promise always to call numbers by their correct place value names."

BRRRRRRRRRRRRRRRIIIINNNGG!!!!

The alarm clock woke Alex with a jolt. Had she really just dreamed all of that? If so, it was some dream! She finally understood Mrs. Googol-Plex's clue! "There's a difference between face value and place value," Alex sang as she got ready for school.

"What have you discovered?" asked her teacher.

"Digits describe numbers," explained Alex. "Numbers describe things. A digit has face value, and a number has place value."

"Good work, Alex!" said Mrs. Googol-Plex. "Remember when we went to the bank? If we put the digit 1 in the hundreds column, that stands for one hundred dollars. If we put the digit 1 in the tens column, that's ten dollars. And if we put in it the ones column, then that's a one-dollar bill."

Mrs. Googol-Plex continued, "If I ask, 'What is the sum of the *numbers* in 123?' the answer is 100 plus 20 plus 3, or 123 ($100 + 20 + 3 = 123$). But if I ask, 'What is the sum of the *digits* in 123?' the answer is six ($1 + 2 + 3 = 6$). Remember, numbers describe how much we have of something."

"Like money?" asked Thomas.

"Correct!" said Mrs. Googol-Plex. "Imagine if I went to the bank and wrote down $123 on my withdrawal slip. I should get 123 dollars. If the clerk gave me six one-dollar bills, I would be upset!"

"I think it's easier to add numbers if you stretch them out," said Alex, "so you can't get confused."

"Show us what you mean by that," said Mrs. Googol-Plex.

Alex walked to the board and wrote:

$$+\$123 = +\$100 + \$20 + \$3$$

$$+\$234 = +\$200 + \$30 + \$4$$

$$\underline{+\$321 = +\$300 + \$20 + \$1}$$

V V V

$$+\$600 + \$70 + \$8$$

V V

$$+\$670 + \$8$$

V

$$= +\$678$$

"Those stretched-out numbers are called *expanded form*," said Mrs. Googol-Plex. "And it's the proof we need to solve our Math Mystery!"

Mrs. Googol-Plex asked everyone to add the equation using expanded notation. "I want to see lots of different ways!" she encouraged.

Thomas added the tens column first, then the ones column, then the hundreds column. "Wait until I show my dad!" he said.

"Good!" laughed Mrs. Googol-Plex.

Wu Li added the ones column, then the hundreds column, then the tens column.

Alex raised her hand. "What do we do when we have to regroup and carry?"

Mrs. Googol-Plex gave a wry smile. "*Carry* is not a math verb," she explained. "Mathematicians count, measure, add, subtract, multiply, divide, rotate, and reflect, but we do not carry. Let's think of things that we do carry. People carry books, bags of groceries, and all sorts of things. But I have never seen anyone carry a number."

Alex thought about that. "So numbers, when used mathematically, are adjectives, not nouns." Then she said slowly, "Numbers describe how much you have of something, the way adjectives describe a noun."

"Exactly!" said Mrs. Googol-Plex. "And you cannot carry an adjective!" She turned to the board with the chalk poised. "Let's try a problem that addresses Alex's question," she suggested. "Does anyone have a kind of noun that you would like to add?"

"Marbles!" said Thomas.

Mrs. Googol-Plex wrote out the following problem:

+ 157 marbles

+ 256 marbles

+ 344 marbles

"Okay, Alex," Mrs. Googol-Plex encouraged, "how many marbles do you get when you add the hundreds column?"

"Six hundred marbles," Alex replied. "May I use the letter *m* instead of writing marbles each time?"

Mrs. Googol-Plex nodded. "Good idea!"

So Alex wrote: 100m + 200m + 300m = 600m.

Wu Li added the tens column next. "Five plus five plus four is fourtee—" she stopped herself. "No, wait! Fifty plus fifty plus forty is 140!"

In her notebook she wrote: 50m + 50m + 40m = 140m.

"Excellent!" said Mrs. Googol-Plex. "Now you're getting it!"

Finally, Thomas added the ones column. "Seven plus six plus four equals seventeen."

In his notebook Thomas wrote: 7m + 6m + 4m = 17m.

+ 157m

+ 256m

+ 344m

600m	=	100m	+	200m	+	300m	Hundreds Column	}	Partial Sum
140m	=	50m	+	50m	+	40m	Tens Column	}	
17m	=	7m	+	6m	+	4m	Ones Column	}	
757m		Final Sum							

"We call this the partial sum of our addition problem," explained Mrs. Googol-Plex. "Now look how easy it is to get our final sum beginning from the left: 600 plus 100 is 700, plus 40 plus 10 plus 7 is?"

"Seven hundred fifty-seven marbles!" chorused the class in unison.

"Wonderful! You are all awesome Math Detectives!" Mrs. Googol-Plex said proudly.

Awesome Alex, Math Detective. Alex liked the way that sounded. She smiled and wondered what her next Math Mystery would be.

Glossary Terms

360 degrees in a circle

The original reason for choosing the degree as a unit of rotations and angles is unknown. An early theory states that it is related to the fact that 360 is the approximate number of days in a year. Ancient astronomers noticed that the sun seems to advance in its elliptical path around the sun by about one degree each day. Some ancient calendars, such as that of the Persians, used 360 days for a year. The use of a calendar with 360 days may be related to sexagesimal numbers. One of the earliest recorded uses of 360 as the total days in a year is found in the Hebrew Bible, Genesis 8-9, which describes the duration of the Great Flood as being twelve months of thirty days each. Many other mathematical theories exist as to why there are 360 degrees in a circle.

Algebra

Algebra (from the Arabic *al-jebr*, meaning reunion of broken parts) is a branch of mathematics that substitutes letters for numbers. An algebraic equation represents a scale. What is done on one side of the scale with a number is also done to the other side of the scale. Algebra uses letters (like n) or other symbols in place of unknown values—for example: $n + 3 = 7$, where n is the unknown (often called the variable).

Amelia Noether

Amelia "Emmy" Noether was an outstanding mathematician. Albert Einstein called her "the most significant creative mathematical genius thus far produced since the higher education of women began."

Noether was born in Germany in 1882 at a time when girls were excluded from schools that put students on a path to university. She overcame many obstacles to earn a Ph.D., and she did significant work on Einstein's theory of relativity. In 1918 she proved two theorems that were basic for both general relativity and elementary particle physics; one is still known as "Noether's Theorem." She did brilliant work in conceptual mathematics in the 1920s but never was able to obtain a university post in Germany, where she was disqualified for being a woman, a Jew, a pacifist, and a left-wing idealist.

When the Nazis came to power, Noether came to the United States, where she got a university post with the help of Albert Einstein. She lived only two more years before dying of cancer at age 53.

Associative Property of Addition and Multiplication

The associative property states that the change in grouping of three or more addends or factors does not change their sum or product. The associative property holds good for both addition and multiplication, but not for subtraction or division.

Examples of the Associative Property

Addition: $(2 + 3) + 5 = 2 + (3 + 5)$

Whether you add 2 and 3 first or 3 and 5 first does not matter. You get the the same sum (10) both ways.

Multiplication: $(4 \times 5) \times 10 = 4 \times (5 \times 10)$

Whether you multiply 4 and 5 first or 5 and 10 first does not matter. You get the the same product (200) both ways.

The associative property gives you permission to add the hundreds column first before the ones column if you wish, and the same holds true for multiplication.

Axis of X and Y

Cartesian coordinates, also called rectangular coordinates, can be used to pinpoint where you are on a map or graph. This method for locating points gets its name from one of the first people known to have used it, the French mathematician and philosopher René Descartes (1596-1650). The Cartesian plane consists of two perpendicular axes that cross at a central point called the origin. The east/west (horizontal) axis is called the x axis, and the north/south (vertical) axis is called the y axis.

Base Ten

In our decimal (base ten) number system, the number dial flips every ten units. After the number nine, we go back to zero and put a one to the left of it in the tens place (10). When the tens place reaches nine and the ones place reaches nine for 99 units, we flip them both to zero and add a one to the left of them at the hundreds place (100). The common belief that we use ten as our system is because we have a total of ten fingers (including thumbs) on our hands.

Base Ten Blocks

Base ten blocks are a mathematical manipulative used to learn base ten place value system.

Calculus

Calculus is the study of how things change. The fundamental idea of calculus is to study change by studying instantaneous change, which means we look at changes over tiny intervals of time.

Commutative Property of Addition and Multiplication

The word *commutative* comes from the stems for "commute" or "move around," so the commutative property in mathematics refers to moving the numbers around. For addition, the rule is $a + b = b + a$; in numbers, this means $2 + 3 = 3 + 2$. For multiplication, the rule is $ab = ba$; in numbers this means $2 \times 3 = 3 \times 2$. Any time a person refers to the commutative property, he or she wants you to move the numbers around using addition or multiplication. The commutative property holds good for both addition and multiplication, but not for subtraction or division.

Decimal

A decimal is a system of numbers and arithmetic based on the number 10, tenth parts, and powers of 10. It is occasionally called the denary system. It is a number that is written with a dot between the part of the number that is equal to 1 or more (a whole number) and the part of the number that is less than 1 (a fraction). For example, the number 423.98 can be written in several forms. In expanded form it is written as 400 + 20 + 3 + 9/10 + 8/100. In multiplicative form it is written as 4(100) + 2(10) + 3(1) + 9(1/10) + 8(1/100). In exponential form it is written as $4(10^2) + 2(10^1) + 3(10^0) + 9(10^{-1}) + 8(10^{-2})$.

Descending Order

Numbers are said to be in descending order when they are arranged from the largest to the smallest. When numbers are arranged from smallest to largest, they are said to be in ascending order. In algebra, arranging numbers from largest to smallest is called the Order of Descending Powers.

Digit

In our decimal (base ten) number system, there are ten digits: 0 through 9. The value of a digit depends on its place, or position, in a number. Digits have face value, whereas numbers have place value. In the number 123, the numbers are 100, 20, and 3, but the digits are 1, 2, and 3. The sum of the three numbers is 123, whereas the sum of the digits is 6.

Ellipse

An ellipse is a shape that resembles a flattened circle or an oval.

Face Value

The face value of a number is the actual value of the digit, no matter the position or place where it sits. For example, in the number 475, the 7 has a face value of 7 but a place value of 70. The 4 has a face value of 4 but a place value of 400.

Fibonacci

Fibonacci is one of the most famous names in mathematics. The Roman Empire introduced Europe to the Roman numeral system, which was not a place value system. In 1202 Leonardo Pisano (known as Fibonacci) published the book *Liber Abaci* in which he introduced the Latin-speaking world to the decimal number system. Roman numerals were not displaced until the mid-thirteenth century A.D., but Pisano's book was one of the first Western books to describe the eventual replacement of the Roman system with the base ten place value system.

The impact of Fibonacci's book as the beginning of the spread of decimal numbers was his greatest mathematical achievement. However, Fibonacci is better remembered for a certain sequence of numbers that appeared as an example in *Liber Abaci*. These are known as the Fibonacci Sequence. The sequence begins: 0, 1, 2, 3, 5, 8, 13, 21, 34, ... In the sequence, the next number is found by adding the two numbers before it.

The Fibonacci numbers are said to be nature's numbering system. They appear everywhere in nature, from leaf arrangements in plants, to the patterns of the florets of a flower, to the bracts of a pine cone, to the scales of a pineapple. The Fibonacci numbers are therefore applicable to the growth of every living thing, including a single cell, a grain of wheat, a hive of bees, and perhaps all of mankind.

Fraction

A fraction (from the Latin *fractus*, meaning broken) represents a part of a whole or, more generally, any number of equal parts. In a fraction, the denominator tells us how many parts the whole is divided into, and the numerator tells us how many of those parts we are talking about. A decimal fraction is a fraction whose denominator is always a power of 10.

Geometry

The word *geometry* is Greek for *geos*, meaning earth, and *metron*, meaning measure. Geometry is the visual study of shapes, sizes, patterns, and positions, as well as the mathematics of the properties, measurement, and relationships of points, lines, angles, surfaces, and solids.

Googol

A googol is 10 to the 100th power. Written mathematically, it is 10^{100}, or the digit 1 followed by 100 zeros. The term was coined in 1938 by nine-year-old Milton Sirotta, a nephew of Edward Kasner. Kasner was a prominent American mathematician and extended the term to the larger *googolplex*. It should be noted that *googol* is the correct spelling of the term, so the spelling *Google* refers to the internet search engine, not 1 with 100 zeros. The googol is considered to be the world's third largest number.

Googolplex

A googolplex is the number 10^{googol}, which is a 1 following by a googol number of zeros. The googolplex is considered to be the world's second largest number.

Googolplexian

A googolplexian is the number $10^{\text{googolplex}}$, which is a 1 followed by a googolplex number of zeros. The googolplexian is considered to be the world's largest number.

Hypatia

Hypatia was the first woman to make a substantial contribution to the development of mathematics. She was one of the last great thinkers of ancient Alexandria, Egypt, and one of the first women to study and teach mathematics, astronomy, and philosophy. She was known more for the work she did in mathematics than in astronomy, primarily for her work on the ideas of conic sections introduced by Apollonius. She edited the work *On the Conics of*

Apollonius, which divided cones into different parts by a plane. This concept developed the ideas of hyperbolas, parabolas, and ellipses. Hypatia's work on this important book made the concepts easier to understand and helped to ensure the survival of the work.

In 415 A.D. Hypatia was killed by a religious mob. Even though her life ended tragically, her life's work remained. More than a thousand years later, Descartes, Newton, and Leibniz expanded on her work. Hypatia made extraordinary accomplishments for a woman in her time, and philosophers considered her a woman of great knowledge and an excellent teacher.

Icosahedron

In geometry, an icosahedron is a polyhedron with twenty triangular faces, thirty edges, and twelve vertices. A regular icosahedron with identical triangular equilateral faces is of geometrical significance because it is identified as one of the five Platonic solids.

Number

A number is an arithmetical value expressed by a word, symbol, or figure representing a particular quantity. It is used to count, label, and measure. In mathematics, the definition of *number* has been extended over the years to include 0, negative numbers, rational numbers, irrational numbers, real numbers, and complex numbers.

Pi

The number pi, denoted by the Greek letter π and pronounced *pie*, is one of the most important numbers in all of mathematics. It is the circumference of any circle divided by its diameter. More simply, it is the number of times the diameter of a circle will fit around the circumference. Pi is one of the most common constants in all of mathematics and is approximately equal to 3.14159.

Place Value

Place value refers to the value of a digit based on its position or place. Place value is often referred to as *positional power* because the position in which the digit sits determines its power.

Semicircle

A semicircle is a half circle, formed by cutting a whole circle along a diameter line.

Stellation

In geometry, stellation is the process of extending a polygon (in two dimensions) or a polyhedron (in three dimensions) to form a new figure. In 1619 Johannes Kepler defined stellation for polygons and polyhedra as the process of extending edges or faces until they meet to form a new polygon or polyhedron. The word *stellation* comes from the Latin *stellātus* or *stella*, which means star.

Tangent

A tangent is a line or line segment that intersects or meets a curved surface at one (and only one) point.

Appendix A

Expanded Form Addition

Original Problem

+ $15
+ $25
<u>+ $36</u>

Labeling the Columns

$10 column $1 column

+ $15
+ $25
<u>+ $36</u>

Expanded Form Notation

$10 $1

+ $15 = + $10 + $5
+ $25 = + $20 + $5
<u>+ $36 = + $30 + $6</u>

Add the Tens Column

$10 $1

+ $15 = + $10 + $5
+ $25 = + $20 + $5
<u>+ $36 = + $30 + $6</u>
+ $60

Add the Ones Column

$10 $1

+ $15 = + $10 + $5
+ $25 = + $20 + $5
<u>+ $36 = + $30 + $6</u>
+ $60 + $10 + $6

Complete the Equation

$10 $1

+ $15 = + $10 + $5
+ $25 = + $20 + $5
<u>+ $36 = + $30 + $6</u>
+ $76 = + $60 + $10 + $6

Vertical Place Value Method and Justification of Work

Add the Tens Column First Then Add the Ones Column

$10 $1

+ $15
+ $25
<u>+ $36</u>
+ $60 = + $10 + $20 + $30 **Partial Sum**
+ <u>$16 = + $5 + $5 + $6</u> **Partial Sum**
+ $76 = + $60 + $10 + $6 **Final Sum**

Add the Ones Column First Then Add the Tens Column

$10 $1

+ $15
+ $25
<u>+ $36</u>
+ $16 = + $5 + $5 + $6 **Partial Sum**
+ <u>$60 = + $10 + $20 + $30</u> **Partial Sum**
+ $76 = + $60 + $10 + $6 **Final Sum**

Appendix B

Algebraic Method: In Terms of Other Numbers

In Terms of Five
Left Hand Side = Right Hand Side

+ 15 = + 3 (5)
+ 25 = + 5 (5)
+ 36 = + 7 (5) + 1
  + 10 (5) + 5 (5) + 1
+ 76 = + 50 + 25 + 1

In Terms of Nine
Left Hand Side = Right Hand Side

+ 15 = + 1 (9) + 6
+ 25 = + 2 (9) + 7
+ 36 = + 4 (9) + 0
  + 7 (9) + 1 (9) + 4
  + 8 (9) + 4
+ 76 = + 72 + 4

In Terms of Twenty-Five
Left Hand Side = Right Hand Side

+ 15 = + 25 – 10
+ 25 = + 25
+ 36 = + 25 + 10 + 1
+ 76 = + 75 + 0 + 1

In Terms of Many Numbers
Left Hand Side = Right Hand Side

+ 15 = + 7 + 7 + 1
+ 25 = + 8 + 8 + 8 + 1
+ 36 = + 10 + 10 + 10 + 6
+ 76 = + 25 + 25 + 20 + 6
+ 76 = + 50 + 26

About the Author

Known simply as Ms. Math to children across the country, Rachel McAnallen has devoted her life to sharing the joy and beauty of mathematics with learners of all ages. Many moons ago, Rachel had a dream about writing a children's math book that featured a precocious young girl. She shared her dream with her niece, Julie Wilder, and after much work and loads of laughter, *Awesum Alex* was born. The book lay dormant for a decade or so and finally came to life after a multitude of revisions. Rachel (Orwhat the Elder) wants to acknowledge her niece Julie (Orwhat the Younger) for helping with the realization of a dream, and as a result, there will be other Awesum Alex math adventures.